BARCELONA

THE CITY AT A GLANCE

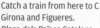

C000053757

Sants Station
Catch a train from here to C
Girona and Figueres.
Plaça dels Països Catalans

Maritime Museum
One of Spain's finest examples of civil
gothic architecture.
Avinguda de les Drassanes, T 342 9920

MACBA
Barcelona's contemporary art museum,
designed by Richard Meier.
See p042

Las Ramblas
A tourist mecca, full of stallholders and
street performers. Head on to La Boqueria.
La Rambla

Park Güell
Gaudí's fantastical park is one of his most
playful creations.
Carrer d'Olot, T 219 3811

City Hall
The centrepiece of the Old City.
Plaça Sant Jaume, T 402 7000

Picasso Museum
See the artist's early work on display
in a row of medieval mansions.
Carrer Montcada 15-23, T 319 6310

El Born Market
Visit the fashion boutiques surrounding
this impressive wrought-iron structure.
Passeig del Born

Sagrada Família
Gaudí's unfinished masterpiece.
See p045

INTRODUCTION
THE CHANGING FACE OF THE URBAN SCENE

In the 1990s, Barcelona set the standard by which every modern city in search of a makeover would like to be measured. The 1992 Olympic Games that it hosted were the most successful of the modern era, and the city became the poster child for urban regeneration and the transformative power of good city planning.

But, arguably, Barcelona became a victim of its own success. As the cruise ships and conventioneers got wise and gradually thronged into town, Barca's distinctive scene began to become, and whisper it, please, a little bit bridge and tunnel. Smarter travellers shifted south to Valencia or across to the Balearics. But they're coming back now, lured by a new breed of hip hotel, the best bar scene in the world, and the innovative and now desperately chic Catalan cuisine.

Flooded with EU migrants from France, the Netherlands, Scandinavia and the UK, Barcelona is far more cosmopolitan now than it has ever been, and no longer just Spain's second city or the Catalan capital but a world-class town. Its already impressive museums have seen the addition of Caixa Forum and the science museum Cosmo Caixa (visit both at www.fundacion.lacaixa.es), while the familiar art nouveau architectural aesthetic is now complemented by a string of new work from a who's who of contemporary international architects. Come to Catalonia, we won't let you put a foot wrong.

ESSENTIAL INFO

FACTS, FIGURES AND USEFUL ADDRESSES

TOURIST OFFICE
Plaça Catalunya 17
T 368 9730
www.barcelonaturisme.com

TRANSPORT
Car hire
Avis, *T 237 5680*
Hertz, *T 902 402 405*
Metro
T 318 7074
www.tmb.net
Taxis
Barnataxi, *T 357 7755*
Fono-Taxi, *T 300 1100*

EMERGENCY SERVICES
Ambulance
061
Emergencies
112
Fire Service
080
Police
091
24-hour pharmacy
Farmàcia Alvarez
Passeig de Gràcia 26
T 302 1124

CONSULATES
British Consulate
Avinguda Diagonal 477
T 366 6200
US Consulate
Passeig Reina Elisenda 23
T 280 2227

MONEY
American Express
Plaça Catalunya
T 902 37 56 37

POSTAL SERVICES
Post Office
Correu Central
Plaça Antonio López
T 486 8050
Shipping
Spain-Tir
T 404 2626
www.spaintir.es

BOOKS
Barcelona by Robert Hughes
(Vintage)
Catalan Cuisine by Colman Andrews
(Harvard Common Press)
Homage To Catalonia by George Orwell
(Penguin Classics)

WEBSITES
Architecture
www.coac.net
www.gaudi2002.bcn.es
Art
www.cccb.org
www.macba.es
www.mnac.es
Newspapers
www.lavanguardia.es
www.elpais.es

COST OF LIVING
Taxi from airport
to city centre
€25
Cappuccino
€2.20
Packet of cigarettes
€2.35
Daily newspaper
€1.10
Bottle of champagne
€55

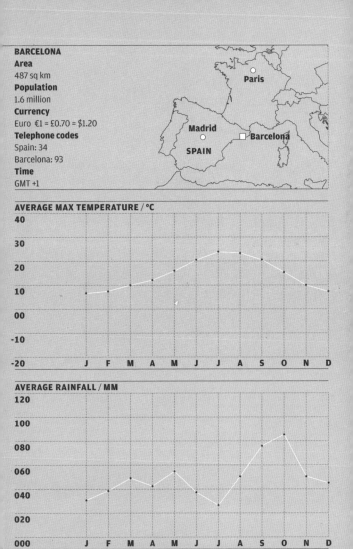

BARCELONA
Area
487 sq km
Population
1.6 million
Currency
Euro €1 = £0.70 = $1.20
Telephone codes
Spain: 34
Barcelona: 93
Time
GMT +1

AVERAGE MAX TEMPERATURE / °C

AVERAGE RAINFALL / MM

NEIGHBOURHOODS

THE AREAS YOU NEED TO KNOW AND WHY

To help you navigate the city, we've chosen the most interesting districts (see the map inside the back cover) and underlined featured venues in colour, according to their location (see below); those venues that are outside these areas are not coloured.

LA BARCELONETA
The man-made beach created for the 1992 Olympics breathed new life into this area, which now bristles with restaurants, bars and modern glass skyscrapers, including Hotel Arts (see p026).

BARRI GÒTIC
The Gothic Quarter is the oldest part of the city, and dates back to Roman times. Its winding medieval streets are lorded over by the flamboyant cathedral.

EL BORN
The Picasso Museum and Textile Museum are both tucked away in El Born's warren of streets. The shopping here is the best in town, although many of the boutiques have now been hijacked by big-name international brands.

L'EIXAMPLE
The well-heeled residential area of Esquerra de l'Eixample to the west of Passeig de Gràcia and south of Diagonal contains some smart boutiques and Sants Station. Gaudí turned Dreta de l'Eixample, the eastern side of the city's 19th-century extension, into a wonderland of modernista icons, including the cathedral, Sagrada Família (see p045), and surreal buildings Casa Batlló (see p044) and Casa Milà (see p014).

GRÀCIA
It is whispered that Gràcia is poised to become the city's next hot area. Boho and pretty, with interesting shops, it is often overlooked by tourists en route to Gaudí's Park Güell.

POBLE SEC
Poble Sec, the area between Montjuïc and Avinguda del Paral·lel, is full of leafy squares and quiet streets. Near the Paral·lel, there are some modernista buildings of note that are worth visiting.

EL POBLENOU
Poblenou is fast becoming gentrified by trendy, loft-dwelling Barcelonians and the fashionable restaurant/club Oven has put it on the map for nightlife.

EL RAVAL
Formerly known as El Barrio Xino, El Raval has swapped its edgy vibe for an arty one, as it is now home to the cultural centres MACBA (see p042) and CCCB, fashionable bars and trendy boutiques.

LA RIBERA
La Ribera is a world away from the boisterous district of El Born, which is located just a couple of streets away. Sedate and sleepy, it still features many small traditional Spanish shops.

LANDMARKS
THE SHAPE OF THE CITY SKYLINE

Barcelona is growing at a dizzying rate. Work over the past five years on the once down-at-heel northern periphery is now pretty much consolidated. The Barcelona Fòrum site (see p077), with its keynote building by Herzog & de Meuron, has become a familiar fact of city life (it is already being used as a kids' playground), while Jean Nouvel's Torre Agbar (see p012), the city's newest symbol, anchors the dotcom neighbourhood at the north end of Diagonal. Architects have long since turned their attentions to Barcelona's western flank, and are now busy remodelling it. Their plans will see part of Gran Via run underground, with a series of plazas and esplanades intended for the freed-up space. This may not be the most prepossessing stretch of the city – El Gornal, the 1970s housing estate still squats over 35 blocks of prime real estate here – but increasingly this is where business visitors find themselves. Not that the city's heart has avoided change. Santa Caterina Market (see p010) serves notice that redevelopment is coming, even to sleepy La Ribera.

In the midst of all this upheaval, it can be comforting to cling to the familiar. Casa Milà (see p014) was Gaudí's first purpose-built apartment block, and offers a gratifying selection of all his signature riffs, for those moments when the summer hawkers and handicams simply infect the Sagrada Família (see p045). *For all addresses, see Resources.*

Santa Caterina Market

A redevelopment initiated by Enric Miralles, and completed after his death by his wife, Benedetta Tagliabue, this colourful, wavy-roofed food market was well worth the wait and its €13m cost. The 68 fresh-produce stallholders retained their original signage, but the design made no other concession to tradition. The surrounding streets were widened to set the market in a grander context and to allow natural light to pour in through the 109 irregularly slatted wooden arches that support the roof. The best views of the market and its rooftop mosaics are to be had from atop one of the neighbouring buildings, but the square makes a good reference point for visitors to La Ribera. *Avinguda de Francesc Cambó, www.mercatsantacaterina.net*

Torre Agbar

Jean Nouvel's 142m tower on Diagonal has quickly become a defining feature of Barcelona's skyline. Unless you are a prospective tenant, it's unlikely you'll gain access to the steel-and-glass interior, but it is easy to appreciate the 4,400-windowed tower from Passeig de Gràcia or Plaça de les Glòries Catalanes. Agbar is the local water company, something that Nouvel seldom tires of referencing in the building's design. This rather sensuous structure resembles a bubbling water stream, and its surface appears to ripple under a liquid film. The top floors are clad in clear glass, while below, metal panels descend in tones of white and blue, before being met by the violent orange, fuchsia and red panels that rise from the base. *Plaça de les Glòries Catalanes, www.torreagbar.com*

Montjuïc Communications Tower

It's hard to remember, but there was a time before Santiago Calatrava had built one of his signature towers or bridges in almost every major metropolis. Fittingly, Barcelona was an early proving ground for the Valencia native, who has subsequently become the world's most crowd-pleasing architect after Frank Gehry. His beautiful communications tower for Telefónica, which was based on

a sketch the architect made of a kneeling figure making an offering, became the public symbol of the Olympic Park during the 1992 Games. Standing 130m high, it certainly cuts an imposing figure, helps delineate the Olympic stadium area and helps steer visitors in the direction of Mies van der Rohe's Pavilion (see p074) just a few minutes walk away.

Estadi Olímpic de Montjuïc

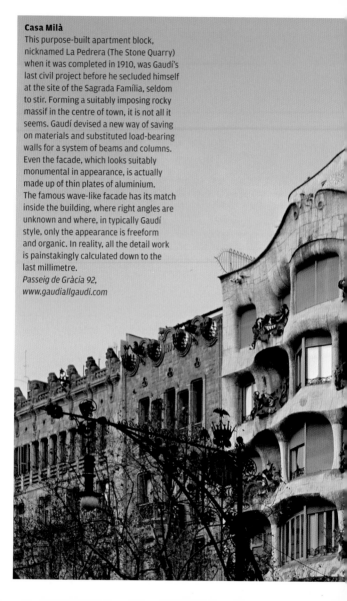

Casa Milà

This purpose-built apartment block, nicknamed La Pedrera (The Stone Quarry) when it was completed in 1910, was Gaudí's last civil project before he secluded himself at the site of the Sagrada Família, seldom to stir. Forming a suitably imposing rocky massif in the centre of town, it is not all it seems. Gaudí devised a new way of saving on materials and substituted load-bearing walls for a system of beams and columns. Even the facade, which looks suitably monumental in appearance, is actually made up of thin plates of aluminium. The famous wave-like facade has its match inside the building, where right angles are unknown and where, in typically Gaudí style, only the appearance is freeform and organic. In reality, all the detail work is painstakingly calculated down to the last millimetre.

Passeig de Gràcia 92,
www.gaudiallgaudi.com

HOTELS

WHERE TO STAY AND WHICH ROOMS TO BOOK

The last few years have seen at least one four- or five-star hotel opening every few months in Barcelona, forcing the city's first design-led properties, such as Hotel Claris (Pau Claris 150, T 487 6262) and Hotel Arts (see p026) to fight that bit harder to attract a well-heeled clientele. While the former still has a loyal following, thanks to its sharp service ethic, the latter has wisely invested in a complete refurbishment and first-class restaurants, including Arola, which serves some of the best modern Catalan cuisine in town. Hotel Omm (see p032) has also jumped on the gastro bandwagon with its hyper-fashionable restaurant Moo (see p054), and Hotel Cram (see p028) has increased its profile by incorporating the legendary restaurant Gaig into its basement.

Looking ahead, the design-hotel boom shows no sign of slowing down. In spring 2006, Derby Hotels opened the four-star Granados 83 (Carrer Enric Granados 83, T 366 8800), offering loft-style rooms in the shell of a turn-of-the-century hospital. This year, AC Hotels opens Palacio de Miramar (www.ac-hotels.com), with 75 rooms overlooking the city on one side and the sea on the other. And November 2006 will see the NH Constanza (www.nh-hotels.com) opening on Diagonal, complete with a Ferran Adrià restaurant. For 2008, W Hotels (www.starwoodhotels.com) is planning a new 475-room property designed by Ricardo Bofill. *For all addresses and room rates, see Resources.*

Banys Orientals

It's almost impossible to get a reservation at this 43-room bolthole. The affordable room rates (coming in at under €100), the elegant interiors by Lazaro Rosa and the location in the heart of trendy El Born have made this hotel wildly popular with visitors who want to be at the epicentre of the city's nightlife but who have only a modest budget. Rooms 211 and 311 have comfortable layouts and look out over the bustling shopping street of Carrer Argenteria. Last year the hotel expanded into the adjacent building, satiating the demand for its rooms with a series of spacious split-level suites. These are highly recommended for shopaholics who need space to accommodate their purchases from the boutiques of El Born. *Carrer Argenteria 37, T 268 8460, www.hotelbanysorientals.com*

Gran Hotel La Florida

Despite being a half-hour drive from the centre of town, this grand property perched on top of Mount Tibidabo is a class act. The rooms are sumptuously furnished with enormous beds and have cavernous marble bathrooms, while the eight designer suites boast unique interiors created by acclaimed artists. The Penthouse Suite was furnished by British artists Ben Jakober and Yannick Yu.

Rebecca Horn is responsible for the Tower Terrace Suite and Cristina Macaya has chosen sensual tones for the Tibidabo Suite (above). Dale Keller's Asian-inspired style graces the Japanese Suite, which overlooks one of the hotel's most impressive features, the indoor-outdoor pool (left and overleaf).
Carretera de Vallvidrera al Tibidabo 83-93,
T 259 3000, www.hotellaflorida.com

Gran Hotel La Florida Pool

Diagonal

Slick and sexy, the Diagonal is the hotel of choice for the design and architecture aficionado with a big-business expense account (it's in the city's financial district with room rates to match). Built in the shadow of the Torre Agbar (see p012), Catalan architect Juli Capella's interiors complement this already iconic landmark, as the public areas, such as the lobby bar (right), are furnished in a sleek, contemporary style. The rooms have the predictable combination of white linen and dark wood, but are saved by fine finishes, high-tech facilities and graphic black-and-white prints that serve as headboards. The views are amazing – rooms 724 and 824 look out onto the Sagrada Família (see p045). The rooftop pool (above) is small, but the sun deck has spectacular vistas.
Avinguda Diagonal 205, T 489 5300,
www.hoteldiagonalbarcelona.com

Neri

This bijou 22-room boutique hotel in the heart of Barri Gòtic is utterly charming. Quartzite-clad bathrooms featuring Etro amenities reflect the design philosophy inspired by the five senses. All rooms ending in 01 and 02 look out onto Felip Neri square.

Carrer Sant Sever 5, T 304 0655, www.hotelneri.com

Hotel Arts

Built as the flagship hotel for the 1992
Olympics, the 482-room Hotel Arts towers
over the beaches of Barceloneta and
Frank Gehry's flying fish sculpture (right).
Thanks to a refurbishment and its Six
Senses Spa (see p092), Arts is once again
the hotel of choice for smart businessmen,
while its three restaurants have made the
hotel a mecca for foodies. Enoteca serves
regional Spanish dishes, while Bites offers
light meals and snacks round the clock.
The best place to dine is Arola, where
modern interiors harmonise with chef
Sergi Arola's contemporary Spanish tapas.
The hotel's Club rooms come with butler
service, Aqua di Parma toiletries and free
food and drink at the Club Lounge. But
it is the 27 apartments with a personal
concierge service and stunning views of
the city that stand out.
Carrer de la Marina 19-21, T 221 1000,
www.ritzcarlton.com

Hotel Cram
As the name of this four-star design hotel in Eixample suggests, the standard rooms are on the small side and depend upon ingenious storage solutions to prevent claustrophobia setting in. It's worth spending a few extra euros and booking a larger room – ask for the Privilege Suite, which has a large terrace and views of Mount Tibidabo and the Sagrada Família (see p045). Basic spa facilities are crammed into a couple of rooms next to the small rooftop pool. Adjacent to the reception, the colourful modern bar with glowing mood lighting is a bold design statement that somewhat sacrifices comfort. But the excellent restaurant, Gaig (above), belies Barcelona's obsession with new-wave Catalan cuisine in favour of a kitchen that serves some of the tastiest traditional local food in Barcelona.
Carrer Aribau 54, T 216 7700,
www.hotelcram.com

Hesperia Tower

This imposing 107m tower, designed by Richard Rogers, has changed the face of Gran Via, the main route from the airport into Barcelona. Conceived as the centrepiece of the city's new 'financial heart', its five-star hotel starts with the airy lobby (left) and spans 27 floors. There are 280 rooms, including a Presidential Suite on the 26th floor, with a private butler and a chauffeur. The impressive amenities (three types of high-speed internet connection, pillow menus and flat-screen TVs in each room) are matched by the excellent Evo restaurant that sits in the glass dome atop the tower. It's headed up by celebrated Michelin-starred Catalan chef Santi Santamaria.

Mare de Déu de Bellvitge 1, T 413 5000, www.hesperia-tower.com

Hotel Omm

The Tragaluz group's first venture into hotels has gone down a storm with the international fashion set, and the city's beautiful people are often to be found draped over the 1950s-inspired furniture in the lounge bar (right). The dark corridors leading to the rooms upstairs feel like futuristic catwalks, thanks to strips of lighting set into the floor. Balconies are ingeniously tucked behind panels of the hotel's facade (above), which looks as if it has been peeled back; those balconies in rooms 501 and 601 offer views of Casa Milà (see p014). The rooftop pool, the Spaciomm spa, with its bespoke products and acclaimed in-house hair salon New Look, cater to the preened and the terminally hip; as does the surprisingly well-equipped basement club Ommsession (see p058).
*Carrer Rosselló 265, T 445 4000,
www.hotelomm.es*

Casa Camper

True to the philosophy of the quirky shoe company that owns it, Casa Camper is eco-friendly (everything is recycled), health-conscious (there's a stringent no-smoking policy) and affordable. Guests can rent the bicycles dangling from the roof in the entrance and whizz round the sites and shops of El Raval, having planned their route with the maps mounted in the mini-lounge that comes with each room.

The architects responsible for Casa Camper have cleverly overcome the awkward layout of the building by creating a green wall of potted plants in the light well (left), which creates a pleasantly verdant vista. There's also a self-service café (above), serving free hot or cold snacks 24 hours a day.
Carrer Elisabets 11, T 342 6280,
www.casacamper.com

Hotel Pulitzer

Located a stone's throw from Plaça de Catalunya and La Rambla, Hotel Pulitzer has 91 rooms, which make up for their tiny floorspace with fabulous interiors and artwork by Lazaro Rosa. Each room has a marble bathroom and three different light settings. Try to reserve room 306 or 506, which both feature leather sofas, high ceilings and cute balconies overlooking Carrer de Bergara. Despite its bijou size, the Pulitzer really packs a punch on the city's hotel scene, especially as it has created a popular bar (right) that attracts a host of trendy Barcelonians on Wednesday and Saturday nights. In summer, everyone heads for the Sky Bar, where local DJs play lounge tracks and sultry bossa nova to complement the stunning night-time views of downtown Barcelona.

Carrer de Bergara 8, T 481 6767, www.hotelpulitzer.es

Hostal Gat Xino

As well as designing the extension to the Thyssen-Bornemisza museum in Madrid, young architectural practice BOPBAA has created simple interiors and a distinctive cat's eye logo for the first two properties in the nascent, no-frills chain of Gat hotels. Hostals Gat Xino and Gat Raval, both in El Raval, offer basic accommodation and minimal service, which helps to keep the prices low.

Gat Xino (above), the larger and better of the two hotels, has 34 rooms, all with en suite facilities, and one suite with a private terrace. The lime-green colour scheme and graffiti-inspired light fittings complement the edginess of the area. There are plans afoot to open more Gat hotels in Lisbon and Madrid.
Carrer de l'Hospital 149-155, T 324 8833, www.gataccommodation.com

Prestige

This four-star bolthole not only has a prime location on Passeig de Gràcia, just a block from Casa Milà (see p014) and Casa Batlló (see p044), but also offers free airport transfers and free parking, making it easy to escape the centre of town. The reception and 24-hour one-to-one concierge service ASK ME are located in a high-tech lounge area, Zeroom (above), which is furnished in exactly the same sober, contemporary style as the 45 rooms. All the superior rooms, except 601 (which is bigger than the rest), have terraces overlooking an internal patio that has been styled like a Japanese garden, with the addition of sun loungers and tables and chairs.
Passeig de Gràcia 62, T 272 4180, www.prestigehotels.com

24 HOURS

SEE THE BEST OF THE CITY IN JUST ONE DAY

Barcelona has such a bewildering range of striking architecture and world-class museums that, on a first visit, even the most organised visitor can only hope to scratch the surface. If you're more interested in the city's heritage than in its architecture and contemporary art, skip MACBA (Plaça dels Angels, T 412 0810) and CCCB (see p042) in El Raval and head for El Born, where the Picasso Museum (Carrer Montcada 15-23, T 319 6310, www.museupicasso.bcn.es) charts the evolution of the painter's oeuvre. Next visit the Textile Museum (Carrer Montcada 12-14, T 319 7603, www.museutextil.bcn.es) opposite, where the shop sells an excellent range of gadgets and one-off garments.

After lunch, head for Montjuïc, where you'll find the excellent Fundació Joan Miró (Parc de Montjuïc, T 329 1908, www.bcn.fjmiro.es) and Mies van der Rohe Pavilion (see p074), a seminal building originally designed to showcase German design and the 'Barcelona' chair. The Fundació La Caixa (Avinguda del Marquès de Comillas 6, T 476 8600; open until 8pm) next door is interesting for its exhibition spaces, which are devoted to science and astrology. At the weekend, make your way to the Font Màgica de Montjuïc (Plaça d'Espanya, T 291 4042; open 8pm-midnight, May to September, 7-9pm October to April), an extravaganza of water jets that dance in time to Tchaikovsky and Abba tracks. *For all addresses, see Resources.*

09.00 Cuines Santa Caterina

Start the day with a croissant, pastry, or *pan con tomate* and *café con leche* at upmarket cantina Cuines Santa Caterina (breakfast served from 8-11.30am). The menus are the table mats, on which dishes are divided into their base ingredients and origin on a bingo-like grid. The dishes arrive in no particular order, adding to the relaxed informality of the place. All the products used have been sourced from the Santa Caterina Market (see p010) that the restaurant calls home, so the Cuines is a perfect introduction to the delicacies on offer. After breakfast, stock up on condiments, chorizos and olive oil, and admire the playfulness of the architecture around you – designed by the late Enric Miralles.

Avinguda Francesc Cambó 16, T 268 9918, www.mercatsantacaterina.net

11.00 CCCB
Be sure to check out the architecture
of this amazing cultural centre before
heading next door to MACBA, the
Richard Meier-designed modern art
museum. Take a minute to admire the
sophisticated graffiti that covers the
surrounding hoardings, then lunch at
the desperately hip Bar Ra (T 301 4163).
Montalegre 5, T 306 4100
www.cccb.org

14.30 Casa Batlló

Walk down to La Rambla, head north to Plaça de Catalunya, then cut across Passeig de Gràcia, where you'll come across Casa Batlló, one of Gaudí's most distinctive residential buildings. Even within this *manzana de la discordia* (block of discord), so called because of its violent clash of architectural styles, the building's extraordinary facade stands out. However, you'll probably be even more taken aback by the surreal, undulating interiors. Highlights include the main drawing room, the private courtyard and the shimmering, tile-clad roof, which is said to represent the dragon slain by Catalonia's patron saint, San Jordi.

Passeig de Gràcia 43, T 216 0306, www.casabatllo.es

16.40 Sagrada Família

Love it or loathe it, Gaudí's cathedral has become *the* architectural icon of the city, despite the fact that it is unfinished a century on. It's predicted that it will still be bristling with cranes for at least another 50 years. Take the lift up one of the 18 towers to admire the blobby spires, wander through the crypt containing Gaudí's tomb and his upside-down mirrored maquettes, then step outside.

The baroque Nativity facade was finished by Gaudí, but the Glory facade, which will depict the life and death of men, is still under construction. When it was unveiled in the 1980s, the Passion facade, with its square-headed apostles and crucified Christ, caused a storm of criticism. *Carrer de Mallorca 401, T 207 3031, www.sagradafamilia.org*

20.30 Sugar Club

After a well-earned siesta, jump into a cab and head to the Sugar Club, a nightclub, lounge and cocktail bar that opens at 8pm. Located in the city's World Trade Center, the Sugar Club offers some of the best views in town and is the ideal spot for a preprandial sundowner (Spaniards wouldn't dream of having dinner until 9.30pm at the very earliest). If you like the vibe here, come back after dinner, when the resident DJs, David Mas and Gustavo Sosa, open up the club and lounge at 11pm. By midnight, both start to fill up with Barcelona's beautiful people. *World Trade Center, T 508 8325, www.sugarclub-barcelona.com*

22.00 Il Giardinetto

In contrast to the hyper-fashionable Sugar Club and the street cafés of El Raval, Il Giardinetto is a classic eaterie favoured by the city's creative establishment. Owned by the same glamorous couple who opened Flash Flash (see p049), the service is sharp and the interiors are appropriately retro, with a fantasy forest theme. The banquettes are teal-coloured and the supporting columns have been painted to resemble giant trees, with canopies of leaves covering the ceiling, which is lovingly retouched every year. As the restaurant's name suggests, the food is Italian. Order the baked brie with marmalade of tomato and apple, followed by *penne alla Sophia Loren*.
Carrer Granada del Penedès 22, T 218 7536

URBAN LIFE
CAFÉS, RESTAURANTS, BARS AND NIGHTCLUBS

As well as its indigenous modernista architecture, Barcelona has developed its own contemporary Catalan cuisine, thanks to the runaway success of El Bulli (Cala Montjoi, T 97 215 0457; open from April to October) further up the Costa Brava. Chef Ferran Adrià has embraced science, alchemy and smell to create tapas that have earned the restaurant a reputation as one of the best in the world, with waiting lists up to a year long. His protégés have opened a slew of similar restaurants in town, including Comerç 24 (Carrer Comerç 24, T 319 2102) and Santa María (Carrer Comerç 17, T 315 1227), which are both cheaper and more accessible. More conservative palates should stick to classic establishments that serve traditional fare, such as 7 Portes (Passeig d'Isabel II 14, T 319 3033) and Can Ravell (Carrer Aragó 313, T 457 5114), where you should book a seat at the marble table downstairs. Alternatively, try the speakeasy-style Tapioles 53 (Carrer Tapioles 53, T 329 2238).

Art aficionados can combine a visit to the Picasso Museum with a meal or a coffee at Els Quatre Gats (Carrer Montsió 3, T 302 4140), which was frequented by the artist at the beginning of the last century. This is where Picasso picked up his first commission, designing the menu. Fans of Gaudí should reserve a table at the excellent Casa Calvet restaurant (Carrer de Casp 48, T 412 4012), which is housed in another distinctive building by the architect. *For all addresses, see Resources.*

Flash Flash

Owned by top 1970s fashion photographer Leopoldo Pomés, this cheap but chic *tortilleria* is a classic, and remains a favourite haunt for Barcelonians of all ages. Take a seat at one of the white leatherette banquettes and admire the walls adorned with stencilled images of Pomés' wife, Karin Leiz. Barcelona's answer to Twiggy, Leiz strikes various poses while brandishing a camera whose flash morphs into the café's light fittings. Tortillas are the house speciality (there are around 50 variations, including sweet ones), but for egg-shy diners the menu offers a selection of burgers, the best of which is the Cadillac Hamburger. Flash Flash does not take reservations, but stays open until 1am.

Carrer Granada del Penedès 25,
T 237 0990

Torre d'Alta Mar
Slick interiors and a 360-degree view of the city and the Med make this Barceloneta fish restaurant, housed 75 metres up in a former cable-car tower, a favourite with the smoother sort of businessmen and, inevitably, with courting couples. Ask for a corner table and order the *suquet*.
Passeig Joan de Borbò 88, T 221 0007, www.torredealtamar.com

Xiringuitó Escribà

Located on Platja Bogatell, this popular beachfront restaurant is renowned for its paellas and *fideuàs* – a paella made with vermicelli instead of rice. If you visit in summer and want to dine alfresco on the terrace, you may have to wait for a table, and even longer for your order to be taken, though your patience will be rewarded by the food and the lively atmosphere. If you're weary of paella, try the vichyssoise with confit potatoes and vanilla oil, sea urchin soup au gratin, or steamed cockles. And do not pass on dessert – this restaurant is run by Barcelona's leading family of pâtissiers. Visit the 100-year-old Escribà pâtisserie on Gran Via (T 454 7535) to sample more of their exquisite cakes and pastries. *Litoral Mar 42, Platja Bogatell, T 221 0729, www.escriba.es*

Cinc Sentits

Chef Jordi Artal and maître d' Amelia Artal are the charming brother-and-sister team who run this Eixample restaurant, which serves modern Catalan cuisine in elegant surroundings. If you want to place yourself in the chef's hands, try the Omakase tasting menu, offered in long or short form, which includes small glasses of wine with each course chosen by the maître d'. If you order à la carte, the foie gras with vinegar-glazed leeks, and lamb cutlets with porcini crust come highly recommended. The Iberian suckling pig served with apples poached in *vi ranci* is another highlight of the menu. Cinc Sentits is gaining a worldwide reputation for its excellent food, so it's worth booking well in advance.

Carrer d'Aribau 58, T 323 9490,
www.cincsentits.com

Moo

Awarded a Michelin star at the end of 2005, Moo is run by the Roca brothers, who propelled the Girona restaurant El Celler de Can Roca to two-star status in 2002. The ground floor of Hotel Omm (see p032) provides a suitably hip setting for this venture, which offers a mix of the sublime, namely a wonderful Catalan tasting menu and the silly – puddings that are named after famous perfumes.
Carrer Rosselló 265, T 445 4000

Negro/Rojo

When it opened in 1999, this split-level restaurant was nominated as a finalist for the esteemed FAD architectural prize. In 2005, the basement was turned into a Japanese restaurant, Rojo, but the original Negro on the ground floor, which serves modern Mediterranean fare, far outstrips its neighbour in culinary terms. Although popular at lunchtime with the finance workers of Diagonal, Negro also pulls in the crowds in the evening, especially from Wednesday to Saturday, when in-house DJs create a buzzing atmosphere that should set the tone for a night on the tiles.
Avinguda Diagonal 640, T 405 9444, www.negrodeltragaluz.com

Ommsession

Hotel Omm's basement club, which opens from 11pm until 3am, Wednesday to Saturday, has a become a mecca for label-clad Barcelonians. Emerging local artists create the projected visuals that appear on the walls. Arrive around 11pm for cocktails in Omm's lobby/lounge, then head downstairs to the club at 1am.
Carrer Rosselló 265, T 445 4000, www.hotelomm.es

Cata 1.81

This tiny gourmet tapas bar, which has bright, slightly stark interiors, has proved a huge hit with trendy locals. 'Cata' means 'tasting measure', and when the restaurant first opened, the wine list of around 250 bottles was the main draw, especially for oenophiles looking to sample as many 25cl decanters as possible. More recently, the wine list has been scaled down and the tapas, such as salt cod with peppers, or fried tuna with caramelised watermelon, are now served as *platillos* – dishes designed to be shared. Be warned, the menu at Cata 1.81 is in Catalan only, and the waiting staff tend to be too busy to stop and translate. It's definitely worth a visit, though.
Carrer València 181, T 323 6818

Noti

The decor in this edgy restaurant/bar in Eixample, which was designed by Francesc Pons, is inspired by *el toreo*, the bullfight. And there is an upbeat, energetic atmosphere in the place to match. The food served in the restaurant is modern European (try the rich fish soup, lobster carpaccio or seared tuna) and the wine list is praised for being well chosen and well priced. If you just want a drink, order a glass of cava at the bar. If you're still there several hours later, you may be joined by a trendy DJ or two. Noti becomes a favourite haunt of the city's beautiful people late into the night, so it's a good place to see and be seen, and perhaps spot a few celebs.
Carrer Roger de Llúria 35, T 342 6673, www.noti-universal.com

Ottimo

This Italian restaurant, which opened in 2005, has an old-school 1950s elegance, thanks to interiors by Francesc Pons and the Sinatra soundtrack that plays while you dine. Well-heeled locals dine on well-executed modern Italian cuisine with Catalan accents. The menu changes seasonally, but you should certainly try the rigatoni Josep Carreras or tagliatelle with truffle oil and poached eggs. For an intimate meal, book a corner table, or if you want to watch the world go by, reserve table three, which looks out onto the street. The bar staff at Ottimo mix a mean cocktail, so we recommend starting your evening with a bellini or two. *Enric Granados 95, T 217 1310, www.ottimorestaurants.com*

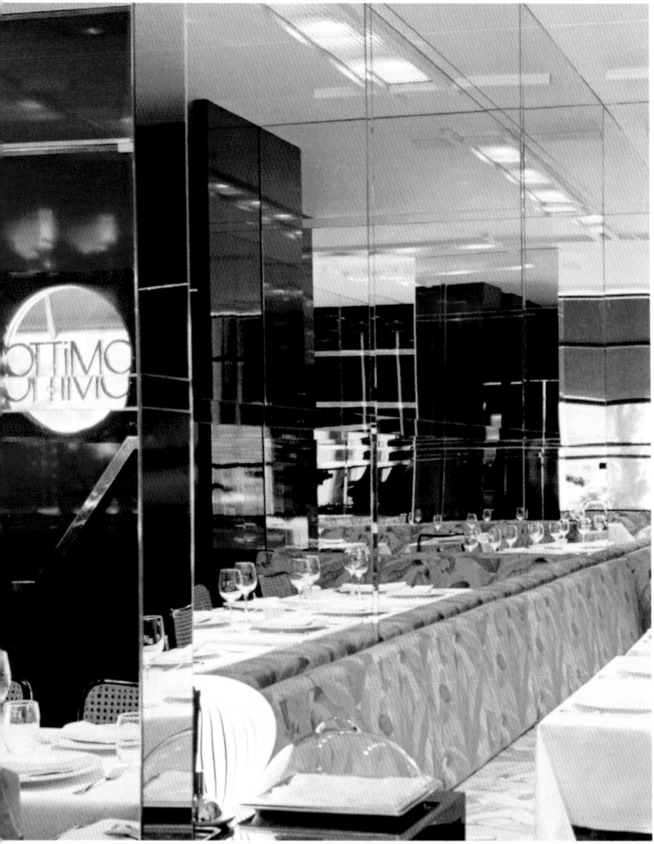
OTTiMO

Abac

Michelin-starred with a modern decor, Abac is a firm favourite with local as well as visiting foodies. Head chef Xavier Pellicer has created an adventurous menu of modern European dishes, such as tarte tatin of eels with apples, artichokes and foie gras, and baby goat roasted with kalamata olives. And the sculptural petits fours will end your meal with an elegant flourish. Table four (above), set in a corner, is best for lunch, while table six is ideal for a candlelit dinner for two. Due to the relentless trendification of El Born, Abac is moving to a more discreet location on Avinguda Tibidabo in early 2007, setting up a Relais & Châteaux-style operation with 16 suites.
Carrer del Rec 79-89, T 319 6600

Club 13

After 11pm, have drinks in the centre of town at Club 13, which attracts a fun and unpretentious crowd. The red and gold interiors and original stone arches create an eclectic environment in which to enjoy a late-night cocktail or a boogie. The house music sessions at Club 13 have a loyal following and attract a long list of well-respected international DJs; stick around if Silvia Prada is on the decks.

When you can shake your tail feather no longer, retreat to the chill-out room, complete with huge, squishy sofas and calming tropical plants.
Plaça Reial 13, T 317 2352,
www.club13bcn.com

Gimlet

This tiny, long-established bar sees trendy rivals come and go, but remains one of El Born's classic destinations. Gimlet serves delicious eponymous gin-and-lime cocktails, with numerous inventive variations created by the highly skilled barmen. It attracts a fashionable crowd of locals and in-the-know foreigners and gets absolutely packed at the weekend, so we recommend calling in on a quieter Wednesday night. This is a classy establishment that you should visit at least once while in town.

Carrer del Rec 24, T 310 1027

És

A turn around El Raval's cute boutiques and temples to cutting-edge creativity – FAD, the centre for art directors and graphic designers (T 443 7520), CCCB, the Contemporary Culture Centre (T 306 4100), and MACBA (see p042) – is bound to build up an appetite. The *plato combinado*, or set lunch menu, at És restaurant (above) is a delicious buffet that costs a mere €10, including a beer or a glass of house wine. Carmelitas (T 412 4684), across the road, serves great coffee, while Lupino Lounge (T 412 3697), round the corner in the shadow of La Boqueria market, is a perfect spot for people-watching.
Carrer del Doctor Dou 14, T 301 0068

Oven

The revamped former industrial district of El Poblenou is teeming with trendy loft-dwelling Barcelonians, who tend to come out to play at this slick bar late on a Friday night. If you arrive in the early evening, have dinner in the restaurant, where you can soak up the lounge music. If you're visiting in summer, ask to sit on the terrace. When the crowds start to arrive, the tables are moved aside to make way for dancing. This venue, which is open on Thursday, Friday and Saturday, attracts renowned international DJs, including Barcelona's most famous spinmaster, Professor Angel Dust.

Carrer Ramón Turró 124-126, T 221 0830, www.oven.ws

INSIDER'S GUIDE

ALEX AL-BADER, MODEL

Alex Al-Bader's modelling career has taken her around the world, from Tokyo to London, but she always finds time to return to her native Barcelona. Her favourite spot for breakfast is the market stall Bar Pinotxo (La Boqueria 466-467, La Rambla 91, T 317 1731; open 6am-7pm, Monday to Saturday), which is located at the entrance to La Boqueria market off La Rambla. When wandering around Barri Gòtic, she suggests stopping for a coffee at either of the two cafés in Plaça del Pi. Her favourite spots for lunch include Cal Pep (Plaça de les Olles 8, T 310 7961) in El Born, which serves delicious tapas, good fillet of beef and sea bass, and the small but atmospheric El Lobito (Ginebra 9, T 319 9164) in Barceloneta, which offers good seasonal seafood for lunch or dinner.

Al-Bader likes to spend her evenings in Barceloneta, calling in at El Vaso de Oro (Balboa 6, T 319 3098) for tapas, followed by dinner at Agua (Passeig Marítim 30, T 225 1272), then cocktails next door at Cdlc (Passeig Marítim 32, T 224 0470). Her favourite clubs include Otto Zutz (Carrer Lincoln 15, T 238 0722), the hip Ommsession (see p058) in the basement of Hotel Omm (see p032) and, on a Friday night, Oven (Carrer Ramón Turró 124-126, T 221 0830), which is in the revamped industrial district of El Poblenou. If you arrive at Oven in the early evening, have dinner in the restaurant, and if you're visiting in the summer, ask for a table on the terrace.

ARCHITOUR

A GUIDE TO BARCELONA'S ICONIC BUILDINGS

Barcelona is in the midst of a long and intense love affair with architecture. It has been here before, of course. The big difference is that a century or so ago its affections were directed at one man, the extraordinary Antoni Gaudí. Today, the city is more profligate with its affections. A single urban regeneration programme – the scheme at Diagonal Mar – attracted the talents of Jean Nouvel, EMBT, Herzog & de Meuron, Dominique Perrault, innovative Dutch architects MVRDV and Josep Lluis Mateo.

Still, a trip to the city would be incomplete without a mini Gaudí tour: Sagrada Família (see p045), Casa Milà (p014) and Casa Batlló (p044), for instance. But if Gaudí's frilly, faux art nouveau isn't to your taste, there are now other options. A visit to Taller de Arquitectura might help make more sense of them. Neither a part of Barcelona's fin-de-siècle architectural past nor a beneficiary of the pre- and post-Olympic Games redevelopment frenzies, it has perhaps been a little neglected. But, in a way, it showcases the lesson that Barcelona has learned over the years. A local architect spent two years remodelling a vast, disused cement factory, and demonstrated in the process the story of today's Barcelona. It's a story of how truly ambitious architecture, such as Torre Agbar (see p012), Santa Caterina Market (see p010) and the Fòrum (see p077) can illuminate the road to reinvention. *For all addresses, see Resources.*

Taller de Arquitectura

A Barcelona native, the architect Ricardo Bofill has built up a practice that produces successful, sophisticated, if seldom heart-stopping, designs all over the world, from a head office for Cartier in Paris to a conference centre in China. For a peek at the firm's idealist past, the cultural centre that serves as its headquarters is hard to beat. A remarkable conversion of an abandoned local cement works, which was completed in 1975, with more than 30 silos, acres of machine rooms and disused subterranean galleries, the Taller de Arquitectura was conceived as a place where engineers, writers, movie makers and philosophers could all hang out and solve the problems of the city. Amazingly, the grandeur of this space does justice to the wildness of that dream.

Sant Just Desvern 14, www.bofill.com

Mies van der Rohe Pavilion

This iconic monument to rationalism, which was built as the German Pavilion for the 1929 Barcelona International Exhibition, became a milestone in modern European architecture. All marble, onyx, chrome and glass, it is the true home of Mies van der Rohe's 'Barcelona' chair. The pavilion was disassembled in 1930, but in 1980, Oriol Bohigas, then head of urban planning at Barcelona City Council, began to appoint a team to research, design and oversee its reconstruction. Ignasi de Solà-Morales, Cristian Cirici and Fernando Ramos were the appointed architects. Work began in 1983 and the new building was opened on its original site in 1986.

Avinguda del Marquès de Comillas, T 423 4016, www.miesbcn.com

Torre de Collserola

Of all the infrastructural improvements wrought by the 1992 Olympics, few were more important to the city's looks in the long term than Foster and Partners' TV tower on Mount Tibidabo. Without the games, there's little doubt that the hill would now be awash with radio masts and TV aerials. Fortunately, the television companies were prevailed upon to combine forces and share this little engineering marvel. Foster managed to house the 288m-high tower on a slender base just 4.5m across. The result is that, while the observation deck offers great views of Barcelona, the view of the tower from the city is almost as spectacular.
Carretera de Vallvidrera al Tibidabo, www.torredecollserola.com

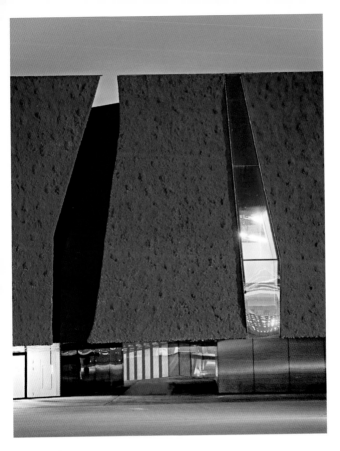

Barcelona Fòrum

Herzog & de Meuron's 2004 contribution to the vast Diagonal Mar redevelopment project is hardly less controversial than EMBT's in the park. At first sight alien to its context, the Fòrum's dissonance actually only grows louder on closer acquaintance. The building was conceived as a sponge, with water running gently down its blue-coal concrete walls, both to reinforce the image and to provide an environmentally friendly cooling system in the summer. Alas, since its opening, teething problems have dogged this vast building, and the reality is rather less elevating and rather more enervating. But for all that, there is a rare beauty, especially on summer evenings, to this otherworldly space.

Plaça Levant, www.barcelona2004.org

Diagonal Mar Park

Initially bitterly controversial, the passage of time and the greening of the site has now made EMBT's park a firm local favourite. It helps that their treatment clearly harks back to the work of the city's favourite son. And while the design of Gaudí's Park Güell arguably dominates its function, here the architecture takes a back seat to a fabulous open space located where the Avinguda Diagonal meets the sea. The park itself consists of six areas, with separate sections for dogs, sports, children and so on, all grouped around the water, which cuts through the site and is punctuated by the architects' remarkable fountains.

Avinguda Diagonal y Cinturón Ronda Litoral, www.diagonalmar.com

SHOPPING
THE CITY'S BEST SHOPS AND WHAT TO BUY

A trip to any cultural or culinary hot spot in Barcelona should always be combined with some targeted retail therapy, as all its districts have a great selection of specialist boutiques. El Born is best for fashion. Head to Como Agua de Mayo (Carrer Argenteria 43, T 319 2330) and Agua del Carmen (Carrer Bonaire 5, T 268 7799) for womenswear, Fet Amb Love (Passeig del Born, T 222 3366) for jewellery, and Lobby (Carrer Ribera 5, T 319 3855) for men's and women's clothes and accessories. Cristina Castañer (Carrer Mestre Nicolau 23, T 414 2428) in Eixample stocks espadrilles with a high-fashion twist, while La Gauche Divine (Passeig de la Pau 7, T 301 6125) in Barri Gòtic sells a host of top Spanish labels.

Foodies should visit one of Spain's best tapas bars, Quimet i Quimet (Carrer Poeta Cabanyes 25, T 442 3142), which is owned by Barcelona's tapas king, Joaquin Perez. Arrive at 7.30pm sharp, before it gets too packed, to sample the menu, then stock up on tinned fish and pickled vegetables, which, in Catalonia, are often considered better than the fresh versions. La Central (Carrer Elisabets 6, T 317 0293) in El Raval is one of the biggest and best bookshops in town. For a smaller selection of tomes on art, design and youth culture, walk round the corner to Ras (Carrer del Doctor Dou 10, T 412 7199). For those on architecture, particularly those on Gaudí, the shop at Casa Milà (see p014) is excellent. *For all addresses, see Resources.*

Recdi8

Hiroshi Tsunoda, one of Barcelona's hottest interior design consultants, undertakes projects from industrial design to smaller domestic commissions. His modular wine rack (above), €350, is in keeping with his approach to furniture design – he's taken a practical everyday item and made it innovative and colourful (this product comes in five colours). The wine rack is the centrepiece of the exquisite collection of furniture, art and objects stocked by interiors boutique Recdi8, which is located in El Born, around the corner from the Picasso Museum.
Carrer Flor del Lliri 4, T 310 6939, www.recdi8.com

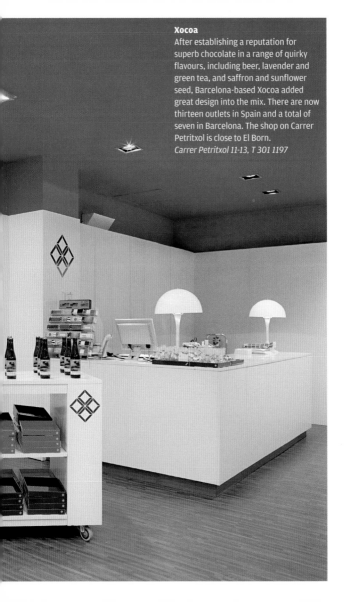

Xocoa

After establishing a reputation for superb chocolate in a range of quirky flavours, including beer, lavender and green tea, and saffron and sunflower seed, Barcelona-based Xocoa added great design into the mix. There are now thirteen outlets in Spain and a total of seven in Barcelona. The shop on Carrer Petritxol is close to El Born.
Carrer Petritxol 11-13, T 301 1197

Vinçon

Barcelona's premier design emporium since the 1960s, Vinçon spans three floors and boasts its own art gallery, roof terrace and show apartment for exhibiting furniture. La Sala Vinçon, which was established in 1973, is a further well-regarded exhibition space. Thanks to a sister shop located in Madrid, and an extensive website offering products to buy online, Vinçon is prospering in the 21st century too. If you are looking for an iconic piece to take home, head for the lighting department to snap up the reinterpretation of the modernist 'Cesta' light (above), €324. Designed by Miguel Milá, the light has a cherry wood frame and opal-white glass shade.
Passeig de Gràcia 96, T 215 6050,
www.vincon.com

Against

The two-floor Against (above) in El Raval is an Aladdin's cave of pan-European furniture, ceramics, plastics, glassware and lighting, dating from the 1950s to the 1980s. For specific requests, you can peruse the extensive website or ask one of the owners to rifle through the dusty shelves of the store's storage rooms. Some of the larger items on sale are also available to rent. Gotham (T 412 4647) in Barri Gòtic is always worth a visit after a tour of the numerous local sites, for its more concise collection of Scandinavian classics and lesser-known mid-century modern Spanish pieces.
Carrer Notariat 9, T 301 5452, www.againstbcn.com

Maxalot

Dutch couple Max Akkerman and Lotje Sodderland's groovy gallery is based on the original concept of elevating graphics and graffiti into an artform by producing colourful, abstract wallpaper that is as much a feature in a room as the furniture. Located in the heart of Barri Gòtic, this small space is devoted to exhibitions of work by some of the world's most cutting-edge creatives. If an image or particular wallpaper catches your eye, a made-to-measure order can be produced. One of our favourite designs is the 'Fuji One' wallpaper (above), from €325 per sq m, by French art director and illustrator Pier Fichefeux.

Carrer Palma de Sant Just 9, T 310 1066, www.maxalot.com

SPORTS AND SPAS

WORK OUT, CHILL OUT OR JUST WATCH

Spain's most popular sport is undoubtedly football, and Barcelona is even more enamoured of the 'beautiful game' due to its two first-division teams. Tickets to watch FC Barcelona (T 496 3702, www.fcbarcelona.com) are like gold dust, but you'll have better luck getting seats to watch the less famous RCD Espanyol (Estadi Olímpic 17-19, www.rcdespanyol.com). Thanks to the 1992 Olympics, the city is well serviced for sports, hosting 17 international events every year, the most famous being the Spanish Grand Prix (Circuit de Catalunya, Montmeló, T 571 9708, www.circuitcat.com), when almost all the hotels in town are sold out.

Barceloneta beach is packed in summer, but it is a perfect spot for an early-morning jog or a stroll before the sun-worshippers descend. For a brisk 3km circuit, start at Hotel Arts (see po26) and make a loop around Passeig Marítim, followed by a circuit around the Parc del Port Olímpic. A more leisurely 2km jog would take you from Hotel Arts up the Carrer de la Marina, turning left at Carrer de Pujades and running round the Parc de la Ciutadella. If the heat is too stifling, head for Carretera de les Aigües in Tibidabo for fresh mountain air and unrivalled views of the city below. If you need a workout, the seven DiR gyms (www.dir.es) are scattered across the city – the most central is near Diagonal (T 202 2202). You will need a passport as proof of ID; a weekly pass costs around €32. *For all addresses, see Resources.*

O2 Centre

This centre for fitness, beauty and wellness is state of the art, and marries excellent facilities with slick interiors, courtesy of architects Luis Alonso and Sergio Balaguer. Many of its spaces have magnificent views of the Parc de Quinta Amelia, most notably the pool, which is clad in black slate in the distinctive style of Peter Zumthor's celebrated spa in Vals, Switzerland. As well as all the usual spa facilities, such as massage and a sauna, O2 offers a wide range of cardiovascular programmes and a well-designed, tailored programme for back problems that aims to cure through preventative exercise. You can even bring your children, get your laundry done, have a haircut, grab a healthy lunch and do a spot of tai chi. *Eduardo Conde 2-6, T 205 3976, www.o2centrowellness.com*

Vall Parc Tennis Club

Vall Parc Tennis Club (above) next to Gran Hotel La Florida (see p018) in Tibidabo has 13 courts, which cost €17 per hour. Serious, semi-professional players should set their sights on the Centre Internacional de Tennis (T 567 7500), which has 35 courts and offers specialised technical, tactical and physical training, on-site physiotherapy, sports massage and all manner of medical assistance. Hard courts here cost €12.60 per hour and clay courts €17 per hour. The centre is a 15-minute taxi ride from La Barceloneta or a five-minute walk from the Cornellà metro stop.

Carretera de L'Arrabassada, T 212 6789, www.vallparc.com

Six Senses Spa
Located on the 42nd and 43rd floors
of Hotel Arts (see p026), this spa is hard
to beat. All the rooms are lit according
to the principles of colour therapy, and
treatments range from hot stone
therapy to the three-hour 'Six Senses'.
Carrer de la Marina 19-21, T 224 7067,
www.ritzcarlton.com

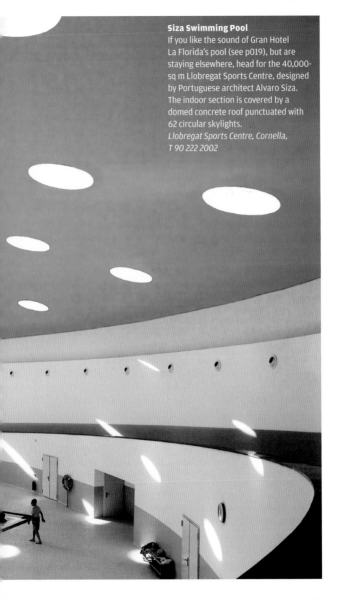

Siza Swimming Pool
If you like the sound of Gran Hotel
La Florida's pool (see p019), but are
staying elsewhere, head for the 40,000-
sq m Llobregat Sports Centre, designed
by Portuguese architect Alvaro Siza.
The indoor section is covered by a
domed concrete roof punctuated with
62 circular skylights.
Llobregat Sports Centre, Cornella,
T 90 222 2002

ESCAPES

WHERE TO GO IF YOU WANT TO LEAVE TOWN

Although Barceloneta beach and the park in Montjuïc provide some respite from the noise and traffic of the city, a day trip to the countryside or the Costa Brava will offer a welcome breather. A visit to the Dalí Museum in Figueres can be combined with the ultimate Spanish culinary experience – dinner at El Bulli (Cala Montjoi, T 97 215 0457; open April to September, booking essential). Ten kilometres northwest of the city, the National Park of Montseny is perfect for a day's hiking, followed by dinner at Can Fabes (Sant Joan 6, Sant Celoni, T 93 867 2851), which also offers cookery courses. The mountains and monastery of Montserrat (www.abadiamontserrat.net) are a must for pilgrims, nature lovers and rock climbers, while Tarragona has Roman ruins declared a World Heritage Site in 2000.

If you need some sea air, head for Sitges or San Pol de Mar. If it's sweltering, the interior of the Costa Brava is cooler than the coast. The countryside of Ampurdan (www.ampurdan.com) has many untouched medieval villages, such as Peratellada, which are lorded over by aristocratic mansions or *masías,* and little-known gastronomic gems such as Mas de Torrent (www.relaischateaux. com). During winter, Vall de Núria (www.valldenuria.com) offers perfect skiing, as it has 10 slopes, glaciers and a ski school. Take a train from Barcelona Sants to Ribes de Freser, then the *cremallera. For all addresses, see Resources.*

Sitges

Sitges, the charming resort beloved of well-heeled and gay Barcelonians, is only a scenic 25-minute train journey from the station at Passeig de Gràcia. Get there early to guarantee a decent space on the beach, then, after a morning of sun, go for lunch at La Nova Estrella (T 93 894 7054). Spend the afternoon wandering through the tiny town's winding streets and stop off at the Cau Ferrat Museum

(T 93 894 0364), the former home of the flamboyant modernista painter Santiago Rusiñol. Enjoy dinner at Al Fresco (T 93 894 0600), before catching the last train back to Barcelona.

Take the C32 toll road south 41km

Wine Tour
Tara Stevens and Kirsten Foster offer bespoke gastro tours for serious foodies. They can whisk you off to nearby villages of culinary note or to bodegas to sample the excellent regional wines of the Penedès. If you prefer going it alone, drive to Bodega Codorníu, where Josep Puig has a spectacular UNESCO-listed cellar. *www.saboroso.com*, *www.codorniu.es*

Cadaqués

Spain's easternmost coastal town sits in splendid isolation behind the Cap de Creus nature reserve, and its whitewashed charm has made it a destination of choice for discerning Catalonians. In the early 20th century, it became an artists' haunt; Picasso painted much of his early Cubist work in Cadaqués, while Salvador Dalí spent his childhood summers here. Dalí and his wife, Gala, bought a cluster of fishermen's houses in Portlligat, which is located 10 minutes north of the centre of town, transforming them into a labyrinthine home. Now a museum, the house offers a glimpse into the lifestyle of the sultan of surrealism. It's advisable to book a tour, as there is only capacity for eight visitors at a time.

Plaça Gala-Salvador Dalí 5, T 97 267 7500
www.salvador-dali.org

Girona/Les Cols

Many visitors to Barcelona resolve to up sticks from their native land and emigrate to the city, only to discover that droves of Europeans have beaten them to it and property prices have become prohibitive. In 2008, Spain's high-speed AVE train will stop in the old Catalan town of Girona (overleaf), where locals enjoy one of the highest standards of living in Spain. The commute into Barcelona Sants will be a mere 20 minutes, making property in town a solid investment. Make an appointment with a local agent, such as Mandarina Houses (T 97 237 4253), and, with a list of preferred properties in hand, reserve a table at legendary restaurant Les Cols (above) for dinner.
Take the A7 north-east 100km,
Les Cols, Carretera de la Canya,
T 97 226 9209, www.lescols.com

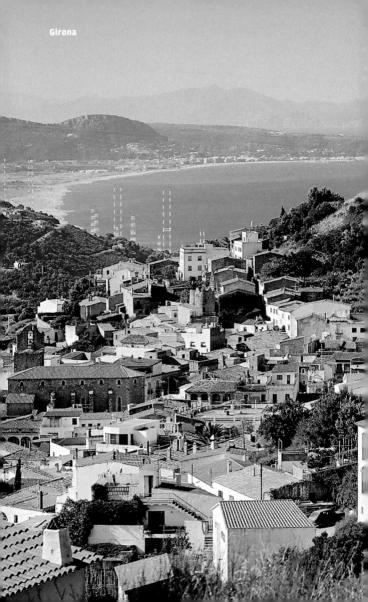

Dear Reader, Books by Phaidon are recognised world-wide for their beauty, scholarship and elegance. We invite you to return this card with your name and e-mail address so that we can keep you informed of our new publications, special offers and events. Alternatively, visit us at **www.phaidon.com** to see our entire list of books, videos and stationery. Register on-line to be included on our regular e-newsletters.

Subjects in which I have a special interest

☐ General Non-Fiction   ☐ Art   ☐ Photography   ☐ Architecture   ☐ Design

☐ Fashion   ☐ Music   ☐ Children's   ☐ Food   ☐ Travel

Mr/Miss/Ms   Initial   Surname

Name

No./Street

City

Post code/Zip code   Country

E-mail

This is not an order form. To order please contact Customer Services at the appropriate address overleaf.

Please delete address not required before mailing

PHAIDON PRESS INC.
180 Varick Street
New York
NY 10014

PHAIDON PRESS LIMITED
Regent's Wharf
All Saints Street
London N1 9PA

Return address for USA and Canada only

*Return address for UK and countries
outside the USA and Canada only*

*Affix
stamp
here*

NOTES

SKETCHES AND MEMOS

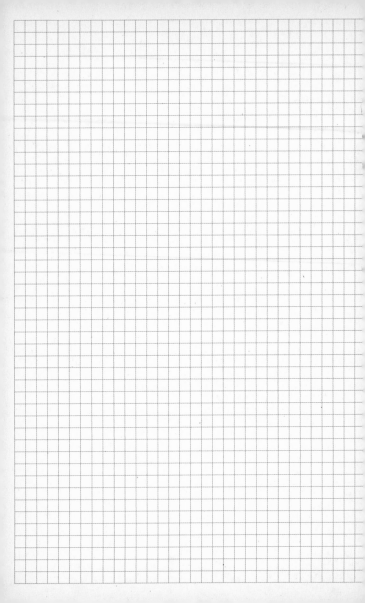

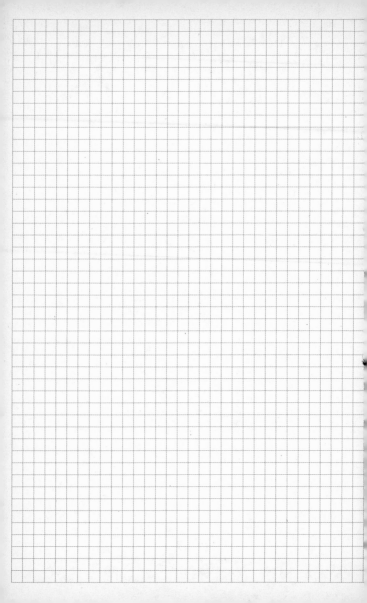

RESOURCES

ADDRESSES AND ROOM RATES

LANDMARKS

010 Santa Caterina Market
Avinguda de Francesc Cambó
www.mercatsanta caterina.net

012 Torre Agbar
Plaça de les Glòries Catalanes
www.torreagbar.com

013 Montjuïc Communications Tower
Estadi Olímpic de Monjuïc

014 Casa Milà
Passeig de Gràcia 92
www.gaudiallgaudi.com

HOTELS

016 Granados 83
Room rates:
double, €231
Carrer Enric Granados 83
T 366 8800
www.derbyhotels.com

016 Hotel Claris
Room rates:
double, €402
Pau Claris 150
T 487 6262
www.derbyhotels.com

017 Banys Orientals
Room rates:
double, €80; rooms 110, 211, 311, €95; suite, €125
Carrer Argenteria 37
T 268 8460
www.hotelbanys orientals.com

018 Gran Hotel La Florida
Room rates:
double, €220-€400;
suite, €600-€2,500;
Japanese, Penthouse, Tibidabo, Tower Terrace Suites, all from €1,500
Carretera de Vallvidrera al Tibidabo 83-93
T 259 3000
www.hotellaflorida.com

022 Diagonal
Room rates:
double, €70-€230;
rooms 724, 824, €70-€230;
suite, €250
Avinguda Diagonal 205
T 489 5300
www.hoteldiagonal barcelona.com

024 Neri
Room rates:
double, €250-€306;
suite, €316-€383
Carrer Sant Sever 5
T 304 0655
www.hotelneri.com

026 Hotel Arts
Room rates:
double, €365-€760;
suite, €485-€1,000;
apartment, €1,200-€2,400
Carrer de la Marina 19-21
T 221 1000
www.ritzcarlton.com

028 Hotel Cram
Room rates:
double, €140-€280;
suite, €245-€350;
Privilege Suite, €220-€310
Carrer Aribau 54
T 216 7700
www.hotelcram.com

030 Hesperia Tower
Room rates:
double, €390-€410;
suite, €470-590;
Presidential Suite, €1,800
Mare de Déu de Bellvitge 1
T 413 5000
www.hesperia-tower.com

032 Hotel Omm
Room rates:
double and rooms 501, 601, €200-€675;
suite, €400-€520
Carrer Rosselló 265
T 454 4000
www.hotelomm.es

034 Casa Camper
Room rates:
double, €200-€235;
suite, €220-€255
Carrer Elisabets 11
T 342 6280
www.casacamper.com

036 Hotel Pulitzer
Room rates:
double, €99-€300;
rooms 306, 506, €160-€300
Carrer de Bergara 8
T 481 6767
www.hotelpulitzer.es

038 Hostal Gat Raval
Room rates:
double, €54-€60
Joaquin Costa 44
T 481 6670
*www.gataccommo
dation.com*
038 Hostal Gat Xino
Room rates:
double, €70-€84;
suite, €100-€120
Carrer de l'Hospital 149-155
T 324 8833
*www.gataccommo
dation.com*
039 Prestige
Room rates:
double, €146-€343;
room 601, €263-€620;
Passeig de Gràcia 62
T 272 4180
www.prestigehotels.com

24 HOURS
040 MACBA
Plaça dels Angels
T 412 0810
www.macba.es
040 Picasso Museum
Carrer Montcada 15-23
T 319 6310
www.museupicasso.bcn.es
040 Textile Museum
Carrer Montcada 12-14
T 319 7603
www.museutextil.bcn.es
**040 Font Màgica
de Montjuïc**
Plaça d'Espanya
T 291 4042

040 Fundació La Caixa
*Avinguda del Marquès de
Comillas 6*
T 476 8600
www.fundacio.lacaixa.es
040 Fundació Joan Miró
Parc de Montjuïc
T 329 1908
www.bcn.fjmiro.es
**041 Cuines Santa
Caterina**
*Avinguda Francesc
Cambó 16*
T 268 9918
*www.mercatsanta
caterina.net*
042 Bar Ra
Plaça Gardunya
T 301 4163
042 CCCB
Montalegre 5
T 306 4100
www.cccb.org
044 Casa Batlló
Passeig de Gràcia 43
T 216 0306
www.casabatllo.es
045 Sagrada Família
Carrer de Mallorca 401
T 207 3031
www.sagradafamilia.org
046 Sugar Club
*World Trade Center
Moll de Barcelona*
T 508 8325
*www.sugarclub-
barcelona.com*

047 Il Giardinetto
*Carrer Granada del
Penedès 22*
T 218 7536

URBAN LIFE
048 Els Quatre Gats
Carrer Montsió 3
T 302 4140
www.4gats.com
048 Santa María
Carrer Comerç 17
T 315 1227
048 7 Portes
Passeig d'Isabel II 14
T 319 3033
www.7portes.com
048 Tapioles 53
Carrer Tapioles 53
T 329 2238
www.tapioles53.com
048 Can Ravell
Carrer Aragó 313
T 457 5114
048 Casa Calvet
Carrer de Casp 48
T 412 4012
048 Comerç 24
Carrer Comerç 24
T 319 2102
www.comerc24.com
048 El Bulli
*Cala Montjoi,
Roses (Girona)*
T 97 215 0457
www.elbulli.com
049 Flash Flash
*Carrer Granada del
Penedès 25*
T 237 0990

050 Torre d'Alta Mar
Passeig Joan de Borbò 88
T 221 0007
www.torredaltamar.com

052 Xiringuitó Escribà
Litoral Mar 42
Platja Bogatell
T 221 0729
www.escriba.es

053 Cinc Sentits
Carrer d'Aribau 58
T 323 9490
www.cincsentits.com

054 Moo
Hotel Omm
Carrer Rosselló 265
T 445 4000
www.hotelomm.es

056 Negro/Rojo
Avinguda Diagonal 640
T 405 9444
www.negrodeltragaluz.com

058 Ommsession
Hotel Omm
Carrer Rosselló 265
T 445 4000
www.hotelomm.es

060 Cata 1.81
Carrer València 181
T 323 6818

061 Noti
Carrer Roger de Llúria 35
T 342 6673
www.noti-universal.com

062 Ottimo
Enric Granados 95
T 217 1310
*www.ottimo
restaurants.com*

064 Abac
Carrer del Rec 79-89
T 319 6600

065 Club 13
Plaça Reial 13
T 317 2352
www.club13bcn.com

066 Gimlet
Carrer del Rec 24
T 310 1027

068 Carmelitas
Carrer del Doctor Dou 1
T 412 4684

068 CCCB
Montalegre 5
T 306 4100
www.cccb.org

068 És
Carrer del Doctor Dou 14
T 301 0068

068 FAD
Plaça dels Àngels 5-6
T 443 7520
www.adg-fad.org

068 Lupino Lounge
Calle del Carme 33
T 412 3697

068 La Boquería
La Rambla 85-89

069 Oven
*Carrer Ramón Turró
124-126*
T 221 0830
www.oven.ws

070 Agua
Passieg Marítim 30
T 225 1272

070 Bar Pinotxo
La Boqueria 466-467
La Rambla 91
T 317 1731

070 Cdlc
Passeig Marítim 32
T 224 0470
www.cdlcbarcelona.com

070 El Lobito
Ginebra 9
T 319 9164

070 El Vaso de Oro
Balboa 6
T 319 3098

070 Cal Pep
Plaça de les Olles 8
T 310 7691

070 Otto Zutz
Carrer Lincoln 15
T 238 0722
www.escriba.es

ARCHITOUR
**073 Taller de
Arquitectura**
Sant Just Desvern 14
www.bofill.com

**074 Mies van der Rohe
Pavilion**
*Avinguda del Marquès
de Comillas*
T 423 4016
www.miesbcn.com

076 Torre de Collserola
*Carretera de Vallvidrera
al Tibidabo*
www.torredecollserola.com

077 Barcelona Fòrum
Plaça Levant
www.barcelona
2004.org
078 Diagonal Mar Park
Avinguda Diagonal y
Cinturón Ronda Litoral
www.diagonalmar.com

SHOPPING
080 Agua del Carmen
Carrer Bonaire 5
T 268 7799
080 Cristina Castañer
Carrer Mestre Nicolau 23
T 414 2428
www.castaner.com
080 Como Agua de Mayo
Carrer Argenteria 43
T 319 2330
080 La Central
Carrer Elisabets 6
T 317 0293
080 Fet Amb Love
Passeig del Born
T 222 3366
080 La Gauche Divine
Passeig de la Pau 7
T 301 6125
www.lagauche-divine.com
080 Lobby
Carrer Ribera 5
T 319 3855
www.lobby-bcn.com
080 Quimet i Quimet
Carrer Poeta Cabanyes 25
T 442 3142

080 Ras
Carrer del Doctor Dou 10
T 412 7199
081 Recdi8
Carrer Flor del Lliri 4
T 310 6939
www.recdi8.com
082 Xocoa
Carrer Petritxol 11-13
T 301 1197
www.xocoa-bcn.com
084 Vinçon
Passeig de Gràcia 96
T 215 6050
www.vincon.com
085 Against
Carrer Notariat 9
T 301 5452
www.againstbcn.com
086 Maxalot
Carrer Palma de Sant Just 9
T 310 1066
www.maxalot.com

SPORTS AND SPAS
088 Circuit de Catalunya
Montmeló
T 571 9708
www.circuitcat.com
088 DiR gyms
Carrer de Ganduxer 25
T 202 2202
www.dir.es
088 FC Barcelona
T 496 3702
www.fcbarcelona.com
088 RCD Espanyol
Estadi Olímpic 17-19
www.rcdespanyol.com

089 O2 Centre
Eduardo Conde 2-6
T 205 3976
www.o2centrowellness.com
090 Vall Parc
Tennis Club
Carretera de L' Arrabassada
T 212 6789
www.vallparc.com
090 Centre
Internacional de Tennis
Carrer Verge de Montserrat
T 567 7500
http://centreinternacional.
fctennis.org
092 Six Senses Spa
42nd-43rd Floor
Hotel Arts
Carrer de la Marina 19-21
T 224 7067
www.ritzcarlton.com
094 Siza Swimming Pool
Llobregat Sports Centre
Cornella
T 90 222 2002

ESCAPES
096 El Bulli
Cala Montjoi
Roses (Girona)
T 97 215 0457
www.elbulli.com
096 Can Fabes
Sant Joan 6
Sant Celoni
T 93 867 2851
www.canfabes.com

WALLPAPER* CITY GUIDES

Editorial Director
Richard Cook

Art Director
Loran Stosskopf
Series Editor
Jeroen Bergmans
Project Editor
Rachael Moloney
Series Retail Editor
Emma Moore
**Executive
Managing Editor**
Jessica Firmin

Chief Designer
Ben Blossom
Designers
Dominic Bell
Sara Martin
Ingvild Sandal
Map Illustrator
Russell Bell

Photography Editor
Emma Blau
Photography Assistant
Jasmine Labeau

Sub-Editor
Paul Sentobe
Editorial Assistant
Milly Nolan

**Wallpaper* Group
Editor-in-Chief**
Jeremy Langmead
Creative Director
Tony Chambers
Publishing Director
Fiona Dent

Thanks to
Paul Barnes
Meirion Pritchard

PHAIDON

Phaidon Press Limited
Regent's Wharf
All Saints Street
London N1 9PA

Phaidon Press Inc
180 Varick Street
New York, NY 10014

www.phaidon.com

First published 2006
© 2006 Phaidon Press
Limited

ISBN 0 7148 4681 3

A CIP Catalogue record for
this book is available from
the British Library.

All prices are correct at
time of going to press, but
are subject to change.

Printed in China

PHOTOGRAPHERS

Palmer Aldritch
Santa Caterina Market,
pp010-011
Torre Agbar, p012
Banys Orientals, p017
Tibidabo Suite, Gran Hotel
La Florida, p018
Hotel Neri, pp024-025
Hotel Omm, p032
MACBA, pp042-043
Casa Batlló, p044
Sagrada Família, p045
Sugar Club, p046
Il Giardinetto, p047
Flash Flash, p049
Torre D'Alta Mar,
pp050-051
Xiringuitó Escribà, p052
Cinc Sentits, p053
Negro/Rojo, pp056-057
Cata 1.81, p060
Noti, p061
Abac, p064
Club 13, p065
Gimlet, pp066-067
És, p068
Oven, p069
Alex Al-Bader, p071
Recdi8, p081
Vinçon, p084
Against, p085
Six Senses Spa, pp092-093

Jeroen Bergmans
Sitges, p097

Montse Casas
Hostal Gat Xino, p038
Roger Casas
Barcelona Fòrum, p077
Diagonal Mar Park,
pp078-079

Gregori Civera
Barcelona, City View,
inside front cover
Casa Milà, pp014-015
Cuines Santa Caterina,
p041
Taller de Arquitectura,
p073

**Gala-Salvador Dalí
Foundation**
Cadaqués Dalí Museum
(images kindly given, all
rights reserved), p100

Ben Johnson
Montjuïc Communications
Tower, p013

**Pepo Segura, Fundació
Mies van der Rohe,
Barcelona**
Mies van der Rohe
Pavilion, pp074-075

Morley von Sternberg
Siza Swimming Pool,
pp094-095

BARCELONA
A COLOUR-CODED GUIDE TO THE CITY'S HOT 'HOODS

LA BARCELONETA
All steel and skyscrapers, this is the brash new town that the Olympics left behind

BARRI GÒTIC
Barcelona's historic heart is lorded over by the flamboyant cathedral

EL BORN
The best shopping in town; somewhere in the jumble of streets is the Picasso Museum

L'EIXAMPLE
This heartland of the modernista movement is the first port of call for Gaudí fans

GRÀCIA
Often ignored by tourists en route to Park Güell, but currently the city's hottest 'hood

EL POBLENOU
The centre of the new nightlife and home to the new generation of loft-living locals

POBLE SEC
For a change of pace, head to the leafy squares and quiet streets of this charming area

EL RAVAL
Now arguably the city's cultural capital, El Raval is packed with bars and boutiques

LA RIBERA
For a sedate vision of the city as it used to be, head here. But do it fast

For a full description of each neighbourhood,
including the places you really must not miss, see the Introduction